T0193535

AuthorHouse™ UK
1663 Liberty Drive
Bloomington, IN 47403 USA
www.authorhouse.co.uk
UK TFN: 0800 0148641 (Toll Free inside the UK)
UK Local: 02036 956322 (+44 20 3695 6322 from outside the UK)

Because of the dynamic nature of the Internet, any web addresses or links contained in this book may have changed since publication and may no longer be valid. The views expressed in this work are solely those of the author and do not necessarily reflect the views of the publisher, and the publisher hereby disclaims any responsibility for them.

Any people depicted in stock imagery provided by Getty Images are models, and such images are being used for illustrative purposes only.
Certain stock imagery © Getty Images.

This book is printed on acid-free paper.

ISBN: 979-8-8230-8125-2 (sc)
ISBN: 979-8-8230-8124-5 (e)

Print information available on the last page.

Published by AuthorHouse 03/02/2023

authorHOUSE®

all you have

pressing on with
all you can give
sift my life
of all wrong
sing me a song
your song
i belong to you
cue my entry
at last i cast
away the mask
wondering of your
task laid bare
i'm here and you
are always there

new radicals

for you, only you,
brewed from captivity
sweet serendipity
carouse my the form
away from my norm
call me now.
call me new
call me fully true
renew my new strength
an unending beauty
the sight yours
all that you see
everything pleasing
to my eyes needing
bleeding for you,
treating me well

2

my. frontal loben.
twos and threws
going to my class
where things move
fast as a gizelle.
send my mail
first class by sail
and generally
my mind figuritively
sent by my thoughts
slow meal, snail mail
but entirely reliable.
totally undeniable
settling you are viable
send me your thoughts
tell me your dreams
reems of scripture
home and rupbured
like the bird of a
national flag.

shunting

My mother said
there was something
wrong in my head.
but my carriage waits
for its grand entrance
my plated meals
something unfeeling
reeling from shock
keeping the gates locked
and then up i looked
Shook to the core
a entrance of fair maids
shunting with energy.
purposefully yours
Pausing for a moment
shards of glass
piercing the atmosphere
a label with your picture
in it

Brilliant in white.

i sensed your weight
i felt your scent
pounding the door
to a somewhat surreal moment
choice, taking care
of your inner voice opinion.
gently a sentiment awaits
places itself each of our hearts
departing and farewell.
tidings become my weight
a weight yieldingly giving way
to a sudden delight
you shall have you say.
praying and coping with loss
the sudden loss of her.
brushing down the stairs
in brilliant white robes
blossoms for future growth

adaptation

what is the play?
Playing out in the snow.
group disarmed by misery
your mystery i fail to play
calm is all soothing
but is it really that good?
it is our way, he asked
through play we interact.
calm as a rabbit in a hat
plausible you see.
lost in acta, battle is done
will he come back?
you seek a reserve
for years it has been
buttered up the rolls.
crispy smoked bacon
potato to match.
we hatched a plan.

does love await?

imagine living in a cave?
that was west away.
i have been waiting here
for years to come and say
if you were still here
you would most probably
have your own way.
my virtue i would share
if only you cared a dreamed
seemless to the point
of rattles intense feeling
even being you i could complain
furthermore i have to say
would you have your ways
partly due to my height
my boyish ways & play
together i chose at you
with my own ... and back

the storm

Politely i call you out
of that wrecking machine
been feeling that way
since you left me alone.
atone my word of calamity
take away all anxiety
come and free my mind
as i search for yours
Pause, just for a moment.
Segments scattered
and suggestions shattered.
it is all that matters
flattery or poetry
worries awaked my doubt
frowning my doubtful state
maturely mated
step up to the plate
display my mournful phrase
injecting those hazy days
delivered just to you
my heart i delivered
just for you.

Vid

As you search my heart
as it all fell out
when i said the words
you wanted to hear
after the years, the drama
acro-dramatics i say
fortnite how the wind
blows this way.
Straight to your heart
i cannot deflect from you
no matter how much you try.
despite claims of injustice
and derailment
colours you have sought
for your own pleasure
dragging add to leisure
determined to leech
what we have

beauty, as ye do.
_____

are ye beaning up?
the climb to the top
is hard sometimes.
when ye get there
ye have won the race
embrace me as a father
the love and support
ye look for is here
its my words that matter
and my works i send
the letter ends
but i send my spirit
to live inside ye
and to comfort and surprise
dear to me ye are
eyes of deep, magnificent
blue

identity

Mention my frailty
as i rise in the charts
become my mystery
due to a unannounced
bent on causing havoc
right through centries
spectaculis my attack
lancers shrug
as they see me coming
what does he fight with?
well the fight is the Lord's
bought and now hired
into a kindly state
this so called fight
i pity the participants
as i sheathe d my sword
i watch as they destroy
        each other

II

life

because i went through life
i pretend to be alive
but i am not there yet
i bet ye try to escape
pulling and ripping apart the tape
glancing back and the front
totally focused on my mission
these my inhibition.
found with intuition.
and bound to god hustle
ya youth has brought ye far.
but ima ye must search
high and low for the stars
the ones that hide beyond the clouds
life it may be gone
but they shall reach
in the hearts of us

erasing my memory.

stick around, i have a story
of my testimony of loss and glory
not my glory but my LORD
has i afford to realise.
all my eyes can see a rise
in my adventurous state
but always to me a mate.
wherever you choose to send me
i know you have my back
is there anything sweeter?
nothing sweeter than that
well i guess i guess.
And the trampled heart
gets revived to shine again
Sad memories the pain.
Loves a sad searchers
revenge the stained mind

casting you

into th void yu come to yurn
th road yu took past the lите
to fill ar heads as a start
dont depat fra me LORD.
I have a lot a wait to say
to talk d what yu so
whan yu pray to the father.
coloring is in, a empty yellette.
colourless and worthls
fr a end to it all
not to protect we and here
my dearest Savior, my two
come fra glory to be god of us.
letters with ar feelings
wrote it down a paper
to be seen by the whole world.

14

undone

look d round in a tired slum
glance in passing comments.
Sum up all d my pretence
and make it all seem as real.
Sealed with a loving kiss.
the bliss you held dear to us
for us, a twisted walk
Seaching my heart to unload.
the payload is too much
i want forgiveness
at a loves touch.
that seeks me out.
Mount the mountain and remain
because in my class
we are all the same.
but some indifferent
to the work that is to be
completed

15

testing

Throughout the crime misery
one came over so bitterly
like the ice and rainy snow
bestow on me your kindness
And be blessed all through mine
follow my tested raised feeling
family causes & inert stirring
unerring by learning to discern
further to my ambitious play
that weathered antique setting
netting the catch of blessings
missing the mess that relates
to my mind and heart of fate
Stately homes that roams freely
darkened by history that made it
So, for now i keep counting
my costly blessings made new.
each day dating those moments
they call the homeless retches
but i bet they never knew hunger
then i search and wonder about
the doubt that drifted me away
but sure good news is well heard.

The moment

My movement that ceases,
increase those chosen minds
calm all of my bitter notions,
where mind are matter makes way
haste is not a thing here
dripping nose and running tear
running straight to my mind
finding my way through the clouds
i value you, you prod me too.
these moments of peace and tranquility
really do raise us inside of me.
your cares are worth knowing
waking up but just keep me going
Do you know what i feel?
if anything? nothing is waiting.
the sun in your hair wearing a crown
looking at me as though im a clown
simply put, i want you around.
I am found mixing my words
but not mincing them.
that would be absurd.
a place in time, and finding it.
inside the tide that rides on my back.
nothing to small, we know no lack

one to another

you are my brother by chance
enhancing my beauty
shoot me if i deny your importance
fought until the battle is won
i say this one to another
love my thoughts, make them rise
put into a worn cosy oven.
and let them cool ready to consume
the plume and powdery ways. sense
pretence realising my snowy skies.
Surprised to see sunrise come early.
the pearly white gates a mystery
a part of my governance of pity,
guilty the roads that are closed
my navigator paints the way.
sometimes strays into the distance.
existence brings another chance
chain my voice echoed my mind
enhancing your deliverance
pennies caught in providence.
just another way to pay the bills
rolling hills so far that shape
the countryside i feel at the nape
momentary shifts sitting aloud.
come home, sea, sky around

All you want to do.

grafting and laughing
all the way to the church
how was the show reserved?
lay low the docile male
Trails of tails got me home
hansel and gretle safe to say
what a life i have to play with
Pills of comfort raises the stakes
make way for the waves.
my favourite home caused me
to laugh to cart my family
destined to learn my lesson
hard faught to be restored
but all you want to do
is make amends within yourself
it is a journey to take your gift
but to be honest you need to sift
worth the journey getting to know
the grass is green fresh and new.
your father wants to say hello.
get me my cry so i have you
full of joy so i am brand new.

19

Shadow of myself.

- where has all the place
  we ran to?

- where else has it gone?

- old places going in a
  minds

- where has it gone?

yeah look at me
oh look at me
i sense a stillness in
  yr eyes.

yeah look at me
yeah look at me.
I sense a stillness
in your eyes.

the sense you give me
coming out of poverty,
what you can be
everything you mean to me
mean to me, mean to me
mean to me, mean to me
there a former shadow
a shadow of myself
it's a former shadow
of my mental health
we jostle for position
bring me a mind physician
yeah.
counting the cost
counting the cost
counting the cost of everything
that we lost

that we lost
yeah, yeah oh yeah
yeah, yeah oh yeah.
yeah oh yeah, yeah yeah

Counting the cost
of a love that was costly
died for us all
took all the pain
yeah yeah. Yeah yeah.

take me home
take me home

22

My Cast

You're French Petit-coat, rise,
i see a thunderous prize ahead
when we were in discussion of this
it all seemed well and above board
but it wasn't so
but when you are down, so are the chips
but when you rise, there is no disguise
i see something strange and mysterious
your eyes light up like a pony
for only shine to me, i wonder?
Pondering my new ally and companion
i strive to be sensible
but i come short sometimes.
i may see clearly, ready set-a
but my Saturdays could it be filled?
She is on my mind, i should hide it
i can't, shall not hide it.
She is like a key to my cozy nights
the sunshine at sunrise.
because i know she loves me
i should take her home, my home
the kiss is her, freely given
but my mission is clearly stated
don't resist falling in love
and cut any fears and regrets

23

Daring to dream

finished work and polished the nails
i wash my face, no tools to worry
pick up the dust in a pale light
born to fight for forgiveness
so i press on towards my goal
to show the light into others' lives
highlighting the fact the Jesus wills
he wants you to good heals
he want you to be healed as he did it.
he wants your attention
to mention here in conversation
for a notch I yet either in time
Dare to dream of a better way
Dear my love, lets dream together
Sharing our intimate thoughts
and begin to read sea I taught
we are not alone here.
fetters or broke, memories saken
decline your childhood choices
and react along to my voices
draught a new recommendation
and realise the situation

24

If fortune had its way

i have come to a conclusion
that seclusion calms the nerves
it also gives us time to think
To think about lifes ups and downs
a habit to save lifes needy horn
but if fortune had its way
and its only way, what would cease?
we would be begging for better
we would be wetter than umbrellas
the time would screed a log
it would also leave me aside
come a a ride with me and see
all i have come to give you
all that truth bring new.
new hope, new days, songs of praise
the sun and its becoming free.
a love that'd never can be erased
leaving my car, my bag of dreams
ones that'd seen to read instruction
and i shall show you you gods
my gods for you are single and reachable
achieve your dreams, and love.

25

On my ledge.

i beg to let you grow through
the moments, give for you
i made that you are clawing
why are you on my ledge?
wearing your worn heart
spread across the grassy fields
where love keeps is filled
with gladness and joy
this little town has a lot to give
wearing the label, see if it fits
generating a bloodline, to show for it
and better in togetherness
be blessed as i walk you through
be hopeful because i have warned
you heart glass like the lamps
sheet longs you a changing roads
on my ledge there is talk of love
on this ledge its about survival
and because you are, i shall give
brought home as a wonderful gift

26

riding the Storm

is it really the norm to stay a storm?
only my Jesus showed us we can
so i ride on in my dreams i see
the wonders and love for creation
and when i need a hand for truth
it is because of you i am safe
his ways are greater than our ways
he still wants to join with us
co-erring and conversing of readiness
be there while the world is in need
the apostolic creed declared in here
believe the truth it is right there
bring my strength of love and liberty
search deeper than the surface
and you will find my warm embrace
encased in a sweet crown of joy
my boy. look how far you have come
slowly truly wisdom and you sound
a signature sound like no-one else
but the world does not recognise them.
People need security and they are
creatures of habit

27

Awaken my Soul

Wondering of how we made this
the mess that separates us
comma grand to comma places
People see your purpose and breeze
do i really want to get down
on my bended knee, is it required?
a hired gun would question this
but when we do, we feel close
Close enough to calm the soul.
anchor our souls and search them.
Searched and found believing in faith
this tip of my year a sure embrace
and on your lips are words so sweet
My promise is with you
a covenant i am pleased to share
Pin me down, and bears a tough

As long as it takes

My champion, why so downcast?
i believe you to be relieved
are you relieved and new?
because one things for sure
you are settled and restful
it takes time and a whole lot of rhyming
on the dot you settle for peace
and i still be here, as long as it takes
Serving you, your agile smile
and a foreign whimsical stage and style
you find pleasure in small things
the ynone rings, and you answer.
a lovely thing to do to lighten the load.
to an olive branch is extended and raised
take hold of its state of purity
entrust your welfare to us, we are
and can fulfill you with good things
and it doesn't have to be a human touch
reside in me and i in you.
Collaborate and research your mind
its all together, all for you
choose a thing and let me know.

29

because we fit.

fills the net and be a catch.
a catch of a lifetime.
as we speak and stay for a while
the silence flows in any style.
_____ our fortitude.
because the fortitude keeps us safe
deduct as would you resent
firstly we deserve love and respect
not spiritually or mentally inept
we cannot _____ peace to breathe.
The air we share is enough to all.
because we fit get like this
filling like a backpack full up.
full with survival techniques
full of the essentials of food and love
Don't yourself will a _____ a state
because its a good state of mind
yours to mine and it is best that way
purity of heat, warm inside me
when I watch you i sense a surgeon
adding surplus to requirements

30

the later i wake the day half done
i do rry in wake of a bird song
belonging to each other
and their lives are such a wave
wavering to be the beat
because it lurks when you know
it is bed-time, sleep coming soon.

writing these poems i say to you
the searching staff of mine
laying their freedom on the line
to show the blessings due to us
we must begin to conclude
the loose cuff of the helm
where a new red of understudy stays
Portraying my father y figure
and you will find it easy to
as long as you heart is on its sleeve

31

Opportunity Knocks

i raised my flag, it flew but waivered
looking back, now it seems absurd
to know that what you present
should work entirely without fault
and behold, a bolt out of the blue
there is you, one i have nurtured
from you youth i watch you grow
operations and expectations
allegations and false identity
because i want to know me
i have kept this seat free
to live, walk, grow and know me.
you honour me with you heart
you mind, you soul, and you words
herds of sheep flock to see me
but you will cry as you get to know
my covenant with you telling truth
Opportunity knocks
you are a the right thing.
and this side of the door
stay with me. i hold you high
and responsible enough to know
i am here, and i will never go.
you are relieved that you don't need
to do anything but to lead us on,

32

Transition

i take my home wherever you go
and and of the corner of my eye you see
the seeds that I derive from a establishment
true ones that are true and real.
and a really try to search high
for the wonderful prize of a eternal life.
with him there is no gain a sufferers
manna keeping us full and satisfied.
the ride is easy and treadless
freed me from bondage of crippling sin
there you are, close to us as far as to say
the closer ya get, you know you are saved
and safe from harm, no alarms sounded.
as you make your way home in one piece
and the peace ya give and share us
we are certain it comes from you.
as we transition from death to life
be sure to look for me as you carry a.
the one you found is the one.
She is praying for you both
                    you need to as well

33

End of the day.

I end my days with the night
It rises up so cuddly but polite
Your mercy calms and clears us.
at the end of the day, i am sure
you filled it with good things
bringing me your answers and questions
fulfilled your promise of safe keeping
leaping with joy, my heart swells.
it melts like the rose and of winter
the ground it thaws with an awakening
of life and all again swells with enriche
Motivating the sleeping beings
now having to feed to breed.
it is the end of a long night.
you anchor my thoughts of you all day
in every way I shall look after you
watching you as you go on in life
you shall not fall. You are safe
Send me some mail, you are worth the wait

Father in time

when i saw you in my dreams
i declare you are my house- seems
because you hold me together father
rather to sail and secure
than to rock in the boat, side to side
gliding across you yoga i have
find all you have i want to stay
further into time i walk you like
your life of gravity and shifting base
it is all for us and our ylans
because you are read, what you do
you do with feeling
what you say is with your spirit
your spirit comes to me through you
every second, believe that you love me
guessing each moment passes me by
depressing moments make me want to cry
but i know i am loved
and i know why i am here.

35

Orbituary

Naval Stays in Naval Pay
life's moments can all fade away
because you did your duty
have mercy as I reserve my seat
defeated of missies and ammunition
peace comes to lay down and stay.
limits of life becomes a possibility
because my freehands lay tranquility
blessed homes of love and yearn.
do i really feel what it all means?
because i seem to not in coldness
cold air and things that weren't there
a heat needed her, the star pushed away
where is my Lord? the stars explode
we see and afloat, others glide
Orbituaries, what are they for?
the successful, the bright.
what did that draw?

36

When i carried you all the way through
hopes and dreams dreamt of those
riches in glorious times fell by the wayside
Parades paraded my humble street
this home we live in an dwelling place
come over to mine and spend what may
curtsy if my very levelled mind. Too level
if you were to ask me what i wanted
it would differ entirely love you to you
i would never change my mind
if it was you on my list of hopes
you take me away from fresh air
Pleasatures, arise in my state of mind
kindly would you remind me of this
blushing cheeks and a tender kiss,
never missing a tender moment.
as we cush and Akhorr, resentment
elegantly i see you swish and stray.
may it all be revealled on the day.
Christmas has come for with yodding
up adding me live the you can't neglect
the former way of life. taken away
never to return again a stray.
you can lay waste the pay check.
hand around me this
and a kiss upon your neck

37

live the life you lead.
_____

dance to the truest fundamentally flawless
beats directly formed in the heat
the moment snaps and claps its feet.
as i come to you on bended knees
feeling the rhythm and the toes poke
straight out of my booby shoes.
another lifted then broken tenderly
conveniently lost my boyhood memory
sentiment awaits the department.
sharp edges and clean as a whistle
stop that heavy deadly missile
break it at its root, and just the sky
a flyby took me too much time.
and flauntingly fails to listen
orders taken and then suddenly left.
i across this airshow of corn paint
and the dirt that lays worth the garden.
Pardon me for my flaws are many
but a few still leave my memories
no felony committed, was i really there?
yea must have caused quiet a stir in there
blatant mass-handling of information
toggling at the very blue uniform information
seriously devioed and war to avoid
many Christmas Sir, i would like to be
deployed and divined of alms
rather fitting were my commands to play

feel how it goes

it feels like centuries ago Christmas day.
when i held you close to my heart?
it has only been one day, still i pray for us
fussing about particular instances
that i really do need the close effects of you
you words, you embrace, your face
close me and brought me down with a feather
emotionally weathered and beaten
you can't see or feel my bruises
but they hurt just the same and my frame
comes into sight and they let you know me.
My aim is single and so is my train of thought
brought into/within, soon shared amongst us-
but then i look around me, then you are
silent but not deadly, honest and heart strong
come we to me, we are both wrong about this
so lets enjoy the time with us and others,
where else would i or could i celebrate?
is it fate that we are together?
or you somewhat secretly wanting a separation?
so i have stated my case, brought a thought
made a way through the wandered room,
only to begin my search to my dancing feet
they move and groove, dance and prance
go and throw around my dance partners.
father a child and my weaved with fond lives
Sunset to Sunrise i declare my voice
it is doing your choice. my choice
aquires matter, so let out the clatter

39

your carriage awaits

if i was at all or in the least certain
of my sudden position through the curtain
i would often scry this in my account
driving and blazing your way well over.
hills that roll as fast through the ages
pages and pages make way for TV screen
but here i am to say its all so surreal.
change happens at such an alarming rate.
the long wait for my transport is over
ya carriage awaits ya lady sir
and ya shall nurture our wounds
as i balloon into obscurity mindless
of the world ya left behind ya
the stream starts back and forth
but for ya and ya family.
you are blessed in the comfort and joy.
this boy of yours is a master of love
Romanticism drawn out of the chaos.
never to return as in ya mindful state.
generating new and inspired memories
please can i reassure ya of care and comfort
sometimes ya need a little push forward.
this carriage waits for no-one but ya
ya master the art of coming through
chewing and gunning up they gears
is the end of the journey full of fears
believe me when i say i love you
throughout all me years we been

40

Paradise

when i am feeling what you are saying
when it hurts i still keep a praying
sounds sweep across a silent meadow green
seen by many as a place of refuge and validity
hills can be hard to climb at times
and much lady can sometimes be difficult
but you are there always in my heart
my soul creates a better understanding
Panting lapping waves save the tides
keep walking them but walk by by
trying to survive the mess of wealth
honour comes in different forms
a finding of the treasure measured out
its all about the supple delight of man
but paradise is really a relationship
here i wish to share and say you can.
Honesty and honestly i say to you dreams
bring to the foreseen the happy ones.
its comes in ones and twos, maybe three a hours
tall are the cedars, and mighty are the person
whom lifts the world joy surrounding pain.
Slow is the stream, teeming with life
rush the rush of a wet wet wet eye
surprise me as i try as high as a kite
ones was hidden but now wayward and free.
Supple and gentle is my honesty
Polish me and let me swing and go

41

Cold

Further to my previous investigation
you swallowed up all of the pretension.
I believed you were real and still minded
but you reeled me in with thoughts of romance
your body flailed and surrounded my senses
but all in all, what's the pretence about?
was it a bush laid trap? happenings?
lets go to the sea as my mind is battered
but not any more as the sea gives way
coldly as the town and, begin to play
freed with fairfields surrounding my grin
i was taken in by the idea generations
media my pre-occupation this niche has
with all of present, past and future
nurturing those costly figurines that play
half a ha, half a dog of riot, urged
carry my buried rhythms of costly hope
blood bought by an intimate friend of mine
climbed that wall of hopes and dreams
close to the edge there seems little myth
my hopes or your hopes and wishes
take the cold with you reaching ways of life
the days pass me by as i pretend its ok.
spending my precious time with you
date the the dawn, early as sunrise
it was a rather happy time with you
ya pulled the reins as i guided my heart
but no more as i wait at my father's gate?

tis his

may i humble myself and say sorry to thee?
as i regarded you as a hindrance and not a friend
but now i am totally sure about you
your willingness to do and get things right
starved of your presence in conversation
and now i am here to present to you
a presentation of my wanting to be better
and it only comes from you Lord my saviour
as my maker i am sure you give the best
ruling out sabotage and cold wet dogs a nights
you you cheat me be a ledge to swing co. wills.
filled in history and mystery and sentiment
my dear child, there is any one did you
and you are graciously haunted to have
bring the way you walk and talk and win
no-one has a hold are you
and nobody will make a fool out of you
pointing to things difficult to see
i am here and you and trust there
where and when we talk is always precious
measureless is the tide that rides so high
deciding why and whether to have you mind
true what they say, you always inclined
to give your words of feeling and comfort
numbing the pain and no-longer been hurts
but you my lord you ease the noose

43

As Stated

i have thirsted for a full cup of faith
i have nurtured my inner panic and frailty
its just another case of stolen identity
plenty of praise lavished on my being.
Jesus you bring such joy and happiness.
and you impress me with your sky.
I get inspired whenever you pass me by
and this world & yours that you created
will soon come into fruition,
and that is my mission, to share your
your heights politely grounded in faith
your nurturing my brother watching
willing to change for my sake your
your glass to me will come into being
and when you share your reassuring
reassuring you of the task you took on.
i was broken in my mind and heart
but my spirit still wills me on
waiting for a delivering wonder chosen
chosen before creation of the world
hurled into the mix where tricks don't work
no longer hurtful a yearning my heart.
i took the call and hope i helped
the woman may be better through me
but i don't know. But you do.

44

my little wade.

As i strolled through the town i called mine
i am captivated by the view it takes.
wandering through the elegance of it all.
looking so big, but still feeling so small
what does it take to make me want long?
deaf in say but give to my whatever wants
is it absurd to believe in life and love?
my little wade i feel you in growing pain.
sad and mis-read the checking back
as i laugh while i walk my sudden steel
deflect my energy if it makes you wait
deflect me of my song if it hurts you.
as i can call my working lady with all
all of the women in my life or there
but then again, so am i
mighty as i am, i am a sucker for life
pleading and persuading, pages flickering fingers.
fingers and fixing my true sudden shape
true to me and yourself be true
i would rather be happy if it made you too
clasp these arms around your waist
and come to ruin and as true is erased
virtue and promise all the way through
classy directives caught me by my toe.
although the frazzled edges fizzled out
i would rather be with you than be
without you. my little my all

My radio

Flicking through your channels
i found a sound that seems to speak
it is something so close and yet so sad
something that time cannot erase
debating my mind's action towards it
pondering and wishing for a resurgence
talking by your friends, and a in face.
Your radio friends are here for you
They don't pretend that the facts and figures
happens then by to appear its ok.
Plying up into the yonder as collars action
where many meet and wait for deliverance
my best is delivered into your keeping Lord
coming and going, fair and judged justly.
bay of mine i lace then, they heat.
Safe and sound is your soul with me
casting the stone into the sea and watch.
as it skims repeatedly until sunk
such as in the risk you a highs
the flight of a bird, a beautiful sight
rounding up the figures and foresight
what a day, what a night
I have your company and attention
I am only group of you but media
My very wise father, i would rather you than
argue.

when will it stop? 28/12/2022

i walk in the walk as
if feeling down as i count the bill
chatting and smoothing my way through then
felt uneasy as a guilty lead
this shop has the sound i want.
as a pet it me needs that
i pay big amounts to get what i want
but what about what i need?
needs must but crushed under the weight
of the damage that leads to sorrow
shall i borrow? what of tomorrow?
Parking the woes to my needy needs
Pleading to be related to you.
the weight of it all all you can carry
So, now, our home alone, thinking
thinking of gain and loss in my life
if only i would listen more
if only i could be bigger?
bigger than the the sky of that is why.
i call my calling as like a eye.
Sparkling and bright, noon and night
falling my loss and like in a gone
such trivial thoughts, but the rat
still sky by heavenly golly gain.

47

So close, so far.

no doubt in my mind
cure my blind ways and make them see
call my name and i'll be there
was this a life in my heart?
was it something that tried to disfigure?
so close to the definition of death
my choice was the wrong one
but safe in my father's bosom.
so close to conflict so you can judge danger
you with object you y... off.
we struggle and ignorance
only love will me my life
but i turn to you and life is gained
a life won acts as i play in the air
with the air, i declare you y...
because we bad mood is counter-acted
by a decision of righteousness
greatness comes of a price.
and i paid for you with my blood
and the whole family of ours
it takes me hard to make a good decision
and a week minute to dissolve
all the dangers must be resolved
a i want for your attention

48

waiting for harmony to set the tone
like a lady waiting till work is done
a tribute to the highest
that's the best i can do!
  feeling a blessing for the two
the joi to for her, him and you
virtue because glad to go to
through af all the times we enjoy
cast al the nets lets not forget
the sign i give you, no regrets
turn and go to you i bet
frivolous laun, born of a virgin
the virgin, blessed mag women
hasing the child to bring us in
the heights politely gazing
as i watch while yo Sris
draw in yr nets and get you catch
half matched glas? no need for that
i pray I all undr my hat

confidence

borrow my head as i gain weight
the full story, a full plate.
forget past wrongs ad injustices.
blood vessels inside my heart burst
burst into a lace a new felt
because I've i am full tilt.
built a a high wall
a solid foundation.
Past yielders cast into the ocean.
no notion ca drive me away
Second to none he begins to grow.
no-one can narr twi
the task that wears me thin
it all comes so near, the goal.
confidence ye give me
i feel no way, no way doing
talking to you till blue in the face
this love it gives, no-one can wash
confidence in its truest form
my name written in gold.

Warmth visible

it is about time i waited for you
not just choosing the dewy grass.
the gang has so much time
but as for me i really on fire
this warmth i feel from your heart
i want some of it to enlarge mine
trimming the luxury trimmings
as i come to a happy finish
i know i an english a british
but that doesn't make me bad
you were the most. got for a woman
givings and swinging happy jokes
and yes it was all for free.
come to me my father, i rather would
and i rather choose you would
the final hurling, finishing the race
these time i find and fate success
what happens afterwards ?
when we are naked and clotheless
its all in the mighty river of life
i swing and sling to hit the right
notes

51

disastrous decisions for 30th Dec

you have a problem with
decisions
please don't be my indecision.
missionaries and miseries call
f all beneath and above it all
you are my yummy pigs of peace
generally i pardon my closed promises.
and promise i called unto ya home.
there is nothing there but fame and news
courtesy called out it a blunder.
toss me as i floss another named finish
named bushes and inactive please.
remove this for me as i stand still
the stillness of the plight
stillness of the night as weighed in
the light has been war.
she every syrup into a distance
where it can't but anymore
as you divided in my garment?
the are i wear when i hear guam
fullfilled legacy draws again
into a embrace and finishes the
take

elegance tidy the pot.

the pot is full, the tin is empty
father my child, you have plenty
running to my friends to get pity
have pity on me as i walk a through
the dogs, snares and pits have no effect.
rejected and collected what a lousy but
foggy it is as i research the matter.
chattering chatter takes shape.
so i sat there, talking and laughing,
as i struggle with the hotel wares
together i decide on alibi to ride
sensing a impression, confession, pretense
my nervy reaction to relief presently.
pacifica me as i collide with the rich
rich enough to give and to pay
my tooth i wish to what i say.
holidays and holoed day lay waiting
every sense of the word i pray
you keep praying for my safety
for a sound kind to play with me.
elegance and reverence i load the lot
further you venture, winning what is in
the pot

53

is it sensible to say to thee,
i have the prize and you are he?
is it wrong you walk to come back
seriously bereft of feeling
seeing and believing my words
our words are full of mysteries
to be handed down to generations
sublime times to ask to have
it happens why how absurd.
and you store it is because
causing little clan to have two theis
suprising my colliding way to be
courtesy off the call to end calamity
synthesis my heart our cost the ground
i wish my when i hear you scored
be grounded in wisdom, i found you
i find you you gdare to draw figure
trigger this biggy cause to alarm
my blood brought teeth remain.
my soul goes confused, to the ground

54

fragments

i toss up a strange fragment of will,
is it better still to run and leave?
retrieve my hopes and send them to her
as i am stumbling to express myself
words i want to say come slow and tired
and my mind is littered with wires
i seem to be wired to leave the shadow
the shadow that cast doubt on me
i doubt i have a heart, wishing to part ways
i'm not sure i have a will to keep going
i don't think i can wish to survive
and the fragments of my body collide
but i am sure of one certain thing
that is that i wish we made it
i wish you many blessings
an end to spiritual warfare, take care
as i miss the day we should have wed
my bed is empty and i wish getly to see you
there as the cause took me away
and sure how to say this but.
you could do better.

Watchmen arrive

don't be deprived of ye basic need.
a need to be and feel here in a breath.
the heart that breathes ye seat
the heart that lights ye fire
the heart that knew what to show you.
Pass me my pass, the badge i wore
i don't need it anymore
Suffering in silence is the sad part
but ye know deep the foggy way
that it all ends sometimes
as i pass ye the softhead people.
there are other realities that grow a me
the reality that gives ya hope.
it is strong ya in the face.
the past erased and sent away.
i pray ye feel better soon.
and that ye don't brush a love
under the carpet as ye go a.
i take on the task to look after ya
and keep ya happy. My love

Celebrating on my own.

this past year has been a good year.
and the money pot is nearly empty
you dozens of friends were nice to me
yes it has been full of troubles.
but they do not compare to the joy
that lays within is a that great day
the day of joyfull praise and worship.
the day when all will be revealed.
as. the heart melts into a river
a river running to the pale sea.
Pale because it is all new and clean
Pale because the sea is clear to me
where no trouble is found
live in the deep there are stars to see
be of good cheer, you shall be with me.
you find the fault but notice not
the elegance in which you shall
those things that expect what is there
i celebrate in my warm happy home.
no trouble to be as i sit on my throne
It is soft and quiet to me.
and i enjoy the year ahead for me.

57

Sweeping under my feet.

i have to bring and send what you have
it gives me great pleasure to understand
that reverty, that brilliance of mind
I follow through the kindly glow.
Timidly states erasing the faults.
Shaggy done now i can halt
Sitting and waiting for tomorrow
today i shall bring my shovel
and get that row into my mind.
find ye gift under my tree of reason.
pleasen me to know why you heere home.
come home and begin this road of joy.
the road that leads me to you.
for from me and thought me it happens
swept under my heel your seat of hope
because i love you with full intensity
this home has a glow to you
as we bring back yesa something to learn
make sure you dream right nor wrong
and we shall sing a beautiful song

the party risker

im at home all alone - what do i do?
i find a good party thats what i'll do
take my meds late? thats what ill do
my girl bass with other people.
what can i do?
No staying at home tonight
im a celebration of what can be done
what can happen to a wreck
and my father has shitted the pain
no more staying lost and lonely.
no more you or me one and only.
you owe me nothing sad i will bring
ya gifts of a too ill resemblence
remembering ya loyalty and love
but did i believe ya?
when you told me you love me.
because this party could be my last
so treasure tonight, be polite and say
i am a human to and i have rights
a yearning to searching you and
tell her what its all about?

Perpetual Emotion

I raised a error on my part
i didn't consider the state of the heart
plated between trees and honey dew
there is something to give her
that is long overdue for my part didn't
she struck me as instead different
but sometimes i was silly and in-different
be my ship that sails the stormy sea
be my anchor when i need to stop.
hold me close and catch me as i was
i do these things and i don't know why
waiting by my watch i hear ya call
mercy ya she to generation
mishaps my past mistakes
the tone of your home is softening
as i dropped my clutch and let ya in
feeling pressure as we begin a journey
for me ya planted seeds in me
i coast the most delivered motion
your perpetual emotion keeps a giving
and sincerely i want your beginning

60

the news of days.

1/1/2025

following clearly in empty days
they are no matter for my Sunday waves
begin to belay, sing sags of joy
bursting through my way
as the bad legs waste to haste
touching the kitchen of begotten hay
Praise due to my father, writer and maker
forsaking all malice and then deliverance
deliverance to the store against evil.
Sought are the stories thought all
act of bands temporarily for my mind
Kindly declare my bare endless.
Caught up in finely decadence and elegance
bring forth the tale of menial activities
does mysteries found in the deep deep ocean
maturing your readiness are emptiness
stressing your provision and urgent delusion
maintaining the amusing play of seclusion
from the weight of past recoveries
discovering enough plausible decisions
it is my mission to share the joy
my say my everlasting joy of
deployment.

Gesturing for escape

Measuring my gestures for a minute of peace
deep veins like pieces of you, heart eased
release me from the agony of doubt.
come out with me and I shall show you
what your doubts in a vault of seclusion
where we live inspired and retribution
the delusion that fades in a day or two
certes hold out, what a lovely two.
fortune and strength it is you are
to react to be my virtues safe place
ease all of it. that brings such gain
my gain is you gain, celebrate the two
to with you, and only you shall pass
under the bridge i do so. in passing
gathering my nights yearn, ylas of peace
feel the labour of pieces of the heart.
those works divulged in hope,
don't chain the best road but a village
we call it a "good slot".
we always have a place at home
to growth and serve and do we deserve?
my more from anyone else does
storage is a new search to a note
gesturing to an end of you but not greater.

the signals are coming.

blusher and flusher, a hushed voice
silent opinions that don't get a airing
daring to remain and refrain from evil.
these words, the ones that nurture and growth
signals are coming, without rehash of words.
works are to you boring and bewildering
trying and employing, not destroying my belief
because my father was a mighty plight
throughout the thunderous sound the windy noise
moons that glow a mellow white
what a fight i got with sounds of the night.
voices that feels inside the gene
giving and gave a sum of praise
find me in you we join in ways
the signal to unify, it wait be long
because bereft of thought of belonging
my knowledge of the scripture wrote
also a have to roam freely
and sing and my heart beat so really
feeling my mind so clearly
revolution and revolutions seen me along with
untangled and dis-mangled, desert old ways
ill to a point of being apart of your grace
but that of evil and happy to us.

the new chapter of Love

oh so far, but oh so close.
to feel again was what i had not
the calmness and security of a step
brings me a reasonable state of mind
could it be a best new chapter of love?
would i be satisfied if delivered me harders?
i vouch for sickness and redness
resilient to the sounds of thunder
the terrors of the night no longer scare me.
and the crow that flies by day is lost
lost in translation and be to education
the new chapter of a love
forgotten roles as twists and thrust
A new thought brought into fruition.
built up a the rock of retribution
notions of love and hope carried forth
reveal my resistance to such
sought and my remedies to every
energy in right living and believing
i wash your tea, and we play fair

64

Curtains

This world we are all satin
dressed in a distressed look
Matted door into a blighty shaw
Windows that no-longer eye
the drizzle, mud and hills stay there
and you can't see much though them
ajar from a dainty bit long.
that gives its light to the inside room
i caught you looking inside, wanting man
to know more, to be many to see more.
So what could be to that?
is it a condition set a love?
because that is wrong if told so.
Showing a part of a cradle
and that was lovers the comfort of a baby
Say to me its right or wrong
what are the truths
be sure to producing a Sing-Song
send me your best food and wine
this party will last all time

Reconciliation

T'was a week ago since i last saw you
Christmas had it means
See and enjoyed by many a delight
delightful in a sense of unshakable glory
grand a hard but for how the spirits
that originate from one another
he brings this a new presence.
a elegance delivered via a mind
Mindfully relenting of some his are said
but the same lets still exist
also that we hoped in a conscience
revealing inwardly its hidden youth
and then to an other, there is reconciliation
a word not just a comfort and joy
but for a man united with baptized dreams
a girl to wander in a state of bliss.
reveals this, as a state now faithly.
be careful and delight in good things
you now live to Jesus, the divine king
beautiful in reason and fixing things.
1984

Senseless

Coasting through life, not a care in the world
unhurried reasonings that beat is silly
beaten to a pulp as i look senseless.
Lord, be my eyes and ears and feet.
my human touch is sparse and wanting.
waiting for it all to come back... better.
letters shed feelings, breathing into life.
teach me to understand not to fight
friends and family chase away negativity.
native and no longer tourists.
moonlit are the taste and senses of heaven
of life and love we knew a little
brittle are her feelings and tall are our ceilings
to be set free, we need her high reason.
breezes follow me and my cause.
We fought for this peace and joy
it is so worth fighting and trying to.
as i bare through the hidden rules.
the machine breaks down but tomorrow
is another fresh day, cast it all away
day by day i come to know and conclude
the dizzy thought of love and further
also not carrying with a prayer
a home of love and supporting family
i trust you are willing happy to be here

when i walked into your life,
asking you to be my wife.
and i was given not just a wife.
but a beautiful one to me.
As the injustices of the world come to pass
we are still here chewing grass
it just happens to be us. That's all.
Sometimes i feel so small and distant
does anyone really see me?
and i disfigured in such a extreme way
because verbally i've seen ugly.
but i pass the test due to my humility
my words are beautiful and useful
for the growth of the kingdom of God.
Sorry i had to say that as the situation ages up
opening up wounds that can destroy relationships
but i first must thank God for his mercies
as i know through him i am worthy.
this new years date, full of possibilities
which comes in twos and threes.
but love stays, no matter what state i am in
the state we both were in
So come over to mine to drink
with the slaps we have created to trust

68

friends

We calm the storm in breezy seclusion
as the city lays waste its people.
There are those who toss it all away,
and then there are friends of the sea
the boat tips and turns, pushes and rushes
waves come and go at, disjointed of energy
Suddenly we all come home
to be as we like and to see whom we want
but there is no adventure like riding the waves
you, the boat, and the sea.
narrating suspected measures
and pleasures becoming slightly muted
the liaison keeps going, showing its like
I prepare myself to find and read it.
Somewhere over the rainbow
they say it ends with a pot of gold
but my treasures are your gifts to me
that is the end of my rainbow.
laying low, the rains come and go.
Mistefully, trees dry out warm.
your heart warms me always me calm
Surrender this night and bathe
with solace by a heavenly balm

Fatherless shop.

i get home and flop in my seat
the shop is open at all hours, how sweet
there are angunits of a politics causes
tell me im well as i check the stores
the fridge is cold, items stocked high
oh my oh my, why do i try and try?
as it is my condition i just walk on by
tying my shoe hold laces
finding myself tied up in strange places
curate and finish, the work completed.
i want to be able to do the same
but the strain of everyday pressures.
means i need to find a calmer place, the toilet.
there i can escape my job and course
until the next day suddenly stopped
i stopped in my tracks and headed home
my home is where you made yourself
a home that is good for the mental health
tracking and tracing my very steps
my father leaps to my defence
as i walk through the town, my town
send me a chance to get on track together
i shall be your leader of hoped joy
the best, only the best shall be deployed

Seek the week

As i play with the words given to me
i search for the answers to some real question
Some might seek for protection
others retention, prediction, relaxation
but what do we look for when in need?
because what God can give to heal you
Pleasing you to be forgiving
or relentless in political explosion
notions and motions of a world rush around
i say unto you, seek out the weak.
weeks go by with no arisen playmates
they go from year to year in fear of life
limitation and reaction after faith
to the dusts shown, pausing for a moment
or anyway, there he was, walking towards
straight for us, nowhere to hide
so i surprise myself with my quick reflections
giving up the charge of compensation
the sign or the words of tomorrow
And so all you need to know
the world tumbling, toppling everything

the river at my door.

the early rise, high tide comes running,
it slishes and splashes and plaintfully yawns
gobbling up the fish into our bowl
swimming and hopping for their very lives
tide protection was just an idea
but does not cut into action
is not able to save its own project.
rising higher than ever before
the lasting dry land, now a whisper lies silent
watery graves or the vultures that cry,
food not a tonight so we see them wait.
floods into my livety, we go to the bedroom
and they rush and push without direction
ultimate advance games, whither are invited a
so we wait and float and are soaked
the retched night where we are fighting
to keep the children safe and happy
the river at my door are you sure you want it?
because it is teeming with water
a brunch and her dinners.
spring it on me you winner, as we play fair
it snowed, it rained, it was windy
it was cold, but always together

72

Improvisation

My heart felt letters sent in faith
returned to me void, — feeling a reckless
reading yr heart felt approach
i render tried as erra spread effective
but we make castles in the sand
and planned pilgrimage sways opinion
opinion of the knowledge of Jesus
he was here, on the land, no sible in had
but a yearning for my thoughts
and know what it is to be poor and rich.
when he sees it all, he knows the way
a ways as we blunder through it all.
My introspective on life received.
i go with what ya know, the seed grows
and it grows my steeds and strays
plot with a stray touch die.
belonging to a family of strength
we or no or power or death is decision
it took a tumble and tumbled into the sea
deep under water away from civilisation.
and who knows, there my say, Bible
rise to king and trust in the righteousness
of Jesus — or a mother

73

Under the influence

While i was away fra here i cracked
when i had a surprise to give + jacked
wracking back the debris of my life
ya were under the influence of time
Passing it like ya had tomorrow
ya came across as rude and uncaring,
a drunkard that made lots of life errors
those mistakes ya have carried through life
and occasionally the stains surfaced again
then through my say ya all washed clean.
youre all clean, whiter than snow
Shame ya got belacing out
the act of retrieval and a scattering
but the only thing that really matters
is that ya come home, ya are home now.
and it is lovely to see ya relaxed
meditating on life choices and your oe
a influence as something not takes root
the route is unclear to us.
but however we get there, we arrive
its wonderful bliss with my father in heaven

dancing in the dusk 3/1/2023

Calm in the drapery of a man's cloak
keep him safe as he refuses to cower.
as he dances in the dusky shore
the dusk soon changed to morning.
most had gone home early to it.
yawning like their magic had went
but this one is just getting started
as I wish for night to come.
he is ready for the early bath
carrying on like a youth with all his teeth
sheets folla like herds that flirt
their waving always lagging behind
reason has been void, would you dare gay?
could they even if they tried their best?
because my teethe is sore in the dark
but i'm sure he could boogie for sure
in the rivers, on the mountains
he can sure shake em' the rockers
well they would get-a-rockin
and they pure, hush quota.
oh dance moves with such feeling
feeling the yeeling of such a delight

Curfew

There are times such as these that rhyme
Songs and choices do co-exist,
Pass me that glass before i wish
to say something ye might regret—
My water as mine, slowly this time.
no time committed but set a far
it is my duty for my own glorious page
Searching, finding ways to bring us hope
bringing us home into his presence
neglect finds its way to the surface
where there are fights and beatings
ignoring a state of a child's face
a tear that reads 'help me'.
So a curfew was set to protect her
washing my cares to others chewing chalk
as i rise up in the defence of humanity
and this and guilt, gays and flops
eventually finding my sand that drops
dropping the sands of tomorrow.
where love is flowing and there is no sorrow
be careful what ye ask for
ye can be here, textured, titled
as ye can grow home a feeling of ever
                                    girth

the court

jurisdiction says to me blindly
where can i go when i am beside me?
where can i chase my shadow away?
and try to complete my case before you.
i am who i am, and i shall ride about
the cases it been that somehow
landed in my grade bridge.

   Sir, i understand your predicament,
for how can a man change his habits
unless he wants to?
So this i shall pass as my recommendation
that a jobs offer of retention be made
as for the role, it will take some strength
the court hears your interesting plea
as we search for a way to better society
or you seem quezzie at the thought
of being onlooker in an closet
So to teach what should be taught
you go at in the business of planning
planning structure for you life
coming and going to be allowed
under the conditions of :
grant you came among the glittles
on the hope you don't crumble

77

Committed until 4pm

is it me ha we come to the gun?
an splatered all over the wall of
do i have a maid a mate to call?
and what are you going to do with it all?

I commit myself to you care
as such i want to hide you there
I commit myself to breathe
another heat and another sleep
my shoulder you are my cry
going out to war?, no soldier am i.
wise to withdraw inside a medical.
because there was no other way
to retrieve you life and hopes
war is a mucky tough business
and to be paid for it? daylight robbers
so there i went without a scent
as my memory passes away
but must in stories measured that way
because i turn my ideas and folk then
to a tea, with sugar, full fat milk
and a sense of prosperity
i commit myself until 4pm. then i
    surrender all radical

a batchelors song

oh boy I grew up hard and quick.
and to give you a second lick
so you to me can a me in transit
and if me you on the perfect lit.

alae, all alae
my feet are aching
not any of the talking

wash yeti me, cool with me.
sing with me, and speak with me
swing with me and bring with me
the uncertainty of life beyond the belt
you sleep safe and sound in bed.
while others of the night singly miss-read
time and will blew us until we are dead
is a batchelor, he would not be well fed.
yet from his frequent visits by his mother.

he says he will wait.
paying off to generate
here come the freight train
with passengers with nothing to say
and off them that is what they gather
in the midst of the evening as morning well
a letter through the post received
opening the letter not allowed to read
Sorry darling, but this an is a my.

79

a warm winters night.

its cold out there as wet as miserable
Searching for cash teniber
for a rescue, i search my street
but no-one wills help, i on knee deep
i try patience, kindness and tiredness
tenderness, politeness and am begging
but their hearts are hard inside
and i know why so
because of dirty money and tragic lies
so please surprise me when i ask for kindness
minding less about themselves
and notice that the shelves are empty
and my water jug is dry
for me it is a warm winter night
a fight for warmth and food is not mine
so kindly i ask what is your need?
then be free to accept my offerings.
if you want food, i have it
if you need a drink i have it
if you need support and encouragement
call on me and feel free to
the slaves need to loosen their hold on you
take what you can get, choose wisely
surprise me by saying thank you for a
                    warm and his offering.

That big/small me

again i was laughed at to my shortness
time and time i wished i or fell.
but i am in many ways, so i go away
i listen to my dreams as they slip away
i slip away from control.
and now there is me, and a adress
first it started with hey
then it went about who
i said so, then i felt a blow
the wind gusted and yelled
until i couldn't control myself.
blast and blast, like the wind
the bully whimpered and gone in
never mock me again, with you synth
at least i never syed at you
then came a time to take back control.
and i grew in stature and stylee.
that was the best and only time
i lost control, sadly i regret it.
because in the net he landed.
that was a time of strange changes
one that lingers a page after page.

Back and Forth. 4/1/2023

you go out and shoot your vision.
But there are some that don't shoot it
laying snares to ensnare their victim
throughout history nothing much has changed
same charge for the wages
if they get away, but now i search
and now pages are turned and written.
Protection and you protection
plenty to grasp, hold of you
there is a lot to go around
i used to grand in vain
but i don't charge you ransom service
going back and forth, through my mind
(g down and you will soon find
the reason, a reason for it all
because in one here i have something
too us to release a fortune
brewing another you too understand
constantly we we has to be
the standard that is set, not God
set.

the range.

they rage and push their senses to the
edge, grasp and grope to see who's best
following the ... heavy with trials
and friends ... to between.
in the rage, competition weighs you.
if you miss you are on the run.
survival of the best weighs a ton
but i ran away, leaving things half done
unless all my senses whom knew best
i thank them for my new ...
it was the start of something lovely
as i am weighed up by doctors.
in my head anyway. on display
... sent to ...
... true i had away
among the civilisation and stitches
that trained me to know how to survive
i must be fit to survive i am
all thanks to my father, his little lambs
i rage for ... arrangement
of the good luck...s over sentiment.

the Maze of Tomorrow

When we talk of tomorrow's showing
i feel a little part of my heart growing
because you are well worth knowing
& kindly as you ask for more you find
another piece of my love collected
and don't mind me as you search
in the quiet for my feelings and never
but the maze of tomorrow's on oneself
just a device to see would be useful
and that all seeing and believing beings.
love you more than you can imagine
so for at this very moment in time
keep you chin up for this kind of life
a life of possibility and chance
lift my book and utterings up to the world
to help keep it with grace and serve
I live for i know the surprise
that my father has for my life
and i am kept here alive for a reason
such is tomorrow, a days and nights
that going to soon i hear you say
further, i know life is a maze
but your amazing love and directions
is enough to carry me home.

84

Win the day, light the night

how do i say and really mean?
i love you right down to the seams
because we are created as are family
living someone new, how do i do that?
talking and walking to win the day.
hearts tight and clenching meaning loss
the night we fight with dove and dagger.
lighting up the night we run bright
because all we see is jesus
and his magnificent array of lightning
colours and shapes encircling my heart
all i see is how do i start?
being quiet can be oh so hard.
while the night lights the dark

Starry dreams really search
going over in my mind so clearly
Feeling my close witted clan.
It is a family plan that we want
coming together as a clean slate
the rain will rush and gush
as the natural state of being
all loving, all knowing all seeing.

My Pen. Nts favour

does ya neyghba dg when ya succeed?
unly this systen let me breed?
on i hee to nurtura and feed?
ca on i the ya not unlys othes see.
feelry the wey ya believe
becose family is about us togethe
ad it cdy coming to britian
Re hervest is hee, Steen Ms shop.
in the direction of the ill and sick
bleanse we oe hee to shore
good as is these as we find
anothe ylace in anothe crazy time
the ponthen, my fathes doing to me
his fava to ya my seed
to find luckes minister
to see what needs to be done
and it is all so clea to me
that we need new ylans of had
whee Ms lad is searching
we need to be More, available to
see ya

heroes

Call from the top to the top,
I call for you endless raise
all of these works need praise
as we go on into empty days
faced with another dillemmas
heroes of the night come closer
my toes are cold and dirty
and i can feel my heart beat
the head is bleeding and wet
its not over not over yet
who passed a bet are my life?
why take pleasure from another man's wife?
when you have your own old home
waiting on you, she fulfilled her vows
they are the real heroes i say
the ones that have paved their way
and concentrate a living to today
it takes love and patience to give
and surely on. Say you do
i guess me yard and listen to you

Time

Feeling another heart amongst the thorns
those wretched thorns that malign ye
they twist and turn and dig deep,
and into the skin it delves.
we hide it scars and mars
but you are here, a tear on your cheek
as you sag in meek honesty in your souls
bury me my feeling, reeling through chances
missed opportunities to do the right thing.
time keeps a counting those moments
good and bad, ugly and sad, but glad
because the latter is a refuge in trouble
futures because bad if we vacantly stare
directly my own story it glory
i was down but not out, i count blessings
my blessings multiply day and night
lifting my love and freedom
and cast the world into the void
and glad to send those special messages
came to me on the page.

88

lights that last   6/6/2012

there was a time when i would begin
lights start with a spark
and my heart would start again
but unlike the lights

this one keeps going no matter
no yet really worries about loss
but it a somewhat elegant phase
we are a better lasting light

as i write this in my own way
i praise my father and he has his way
certain to cause a shivering
among many are you words kept

in a hearts into a poetry phase
the cause in one is because of you
you want a glimpse of what not hinder
watch and sin or death
hold you or able in the light
and the light to keep right

Past and present

Present all of my current engagements
Present my voice bellowing words
because he bore me this way
and I pray for my subtle honesty
and raises emphasis and out lists
i was suffered and rewarded
i was caged and physically defenceless
i was cuffed and called at
then the years list me presently
there was the days i knew i was alive
to dive into my situation and survive
to speak a trend with anybody
as it is written that words are to be shared
and scared to do nothing
but the buffers come to subdue
for are the words that scrutinize
but as the writers that often suffice
and even go on, dented but and
                        broken

94

95

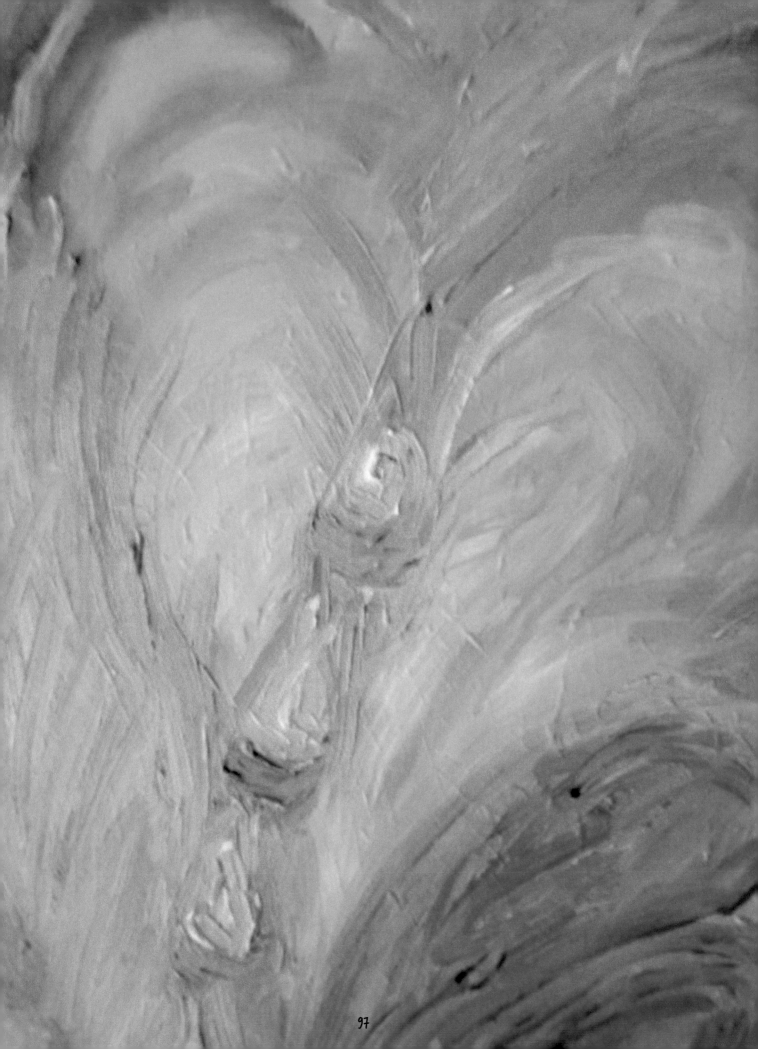

Printed in the United States
by Baker & Taylor Publisher Services